QUALITY
RESTAURANT
SERVICE
GUARANTEED

QUALITY RESTAURANT SERVICE GUARANTEED

A Training Outline

Nancy Loman Scanlon

JOHN WILEY & SONS, INC.

New York • Chichester • Weinheim • Singapore • Toronto

This book is printed on acid-free paper. ∞

Copyright ©1998 by John Wiley & Sons, Inc. All rights reserved.

Published simultaneously in Canada.

This publication is designed to provide accurate and authoritative information in regard to the
subject matter covered. It is sold with the understanding that the publisher is not engaged in
rendering professional services. If professional advice or other expert assistance is required, the
services of a competent professional person should be sought.

Library of Congress Cataloging-in-Publication Data:
Scanlon, Nancy Loman.
   Quality Restaurant Service Guaranteed: a training outline/Nancy Loman
Scanlon.
       p.cm.
    Includes index.
     ISBN 0-471-02852-5 (cloth: alk. paper)
     1. Foodservice—Quality control. 2. Total quality management.
3. Restaurants—Employees—Training of. I. Title.
TX911.3.Q34S33 1998
642'.5'0715—dc21   98-4730

Printed in the United States of America.

10 9 8 7 6 5 4 3 2 1

For Gertrude, whose phenomenal attitude makes us all feel like "Quality."

CONTENTS

PREFACE

The objective of "Quality Restaurant Service Guaranteed" is to provide foodservice operators with a basic format for a quality service program that is easily adapted to their operation with a minimum of time, cost, and frustration.

This book offers an outline of successful quality service steps as they are applied in different styles of foodservice operations:

- Quick service

- Casual family style service

- All purpose casual service

- Full-service, Bistro style

- Full-service, traditional

Critical paths of service for each of these operations are offered as potential blueprints from which to develop service programs for your organization. Total Quality Service (TQS) points identify areas of the service path to which value-added service techniques can be added. Value-added service techniques give the customers more than what they paid for a particular menu item or service.

The level of service that customers expect from a foodservice operation will depend on the atmosphere, concept, menu item selection, level of food quality, and price. The level of quality service offered at McDonald's is certainly far less than the level of service offered at a Houston's or an Olive Garden Italian Restaurant. Customers at McDonald's don't expect the same level of service for the price of a McDonald's cheeseburger that they expect for the price of a steak dinner at Houston's, but they do expect a certain level of quality, and that level must be identified and met. Even more important, the level of quality must be consistent every time a customer patronizes the foodservice operation. Many of the exercises in this book discuss marketing practices to identify customer needs and expectations, along with ideas on how to meet them.

No matter how well-intentioned and determined you are to inform yourself about how to become truly successful in today's marketplace, more often than not you will find yourself deterred by the simple day-to-day functions of trying to run your business. The result is that it may seem impossible to design and implement a Quality Service Program specific to your business without seeking the assistance of outside consultants and/or management teams within your organization.

Quality Restaurant Service Guaranteed provides this assistance, giving you the blueprints on which to build a Quality Service Program for the five major styles of foodservice operations featured. Beginning with an identification of the basic levels of service required for the various styles of foodservice operation, the book goes on to define a series of critical paths of service, blueprints you can use to develop a quality service program at the level you feel is appropriate for your individual operation.

ACKNOWLEDGMENTS

Without the support and assistance of the owners, management, and service staff of the restaurants used as examples for the "Creating Quality Service" segment of this book, *Quality Restaurant Service Guaranteed* would not have been possible. My sincere gratitude and appreciation to Dominick Pulieri, owner of Grotto Restaurants Incorporated and Beverly Cox, Executive Assistant; to Marcia Brown, manager of Ruth Chris, Philadelphia, and her most willing and able staff; to the Manhattan Beach Marriott and the Garden Restaurant staff; to Sally Rogers, Senior Trainer, Au Bon Pain and the staff of the Harvard Square, Boston, Au Bon Pain location; and to the Matos brothers, Al and Eduardo, along with the management of The Reunion Inn & Grill in Camden, Maine.

For their generosity in lending their restaurants, resources, and their staffs for this effort, thank you.

NANCY LOMAN SCANLON

1

QUALITY SERVICE
SUCCESS STORIES

T he search for quality service in American industry is evident in the success of such diverse businesses as Wal-Mart, American Airlines, Nordstrom's, United Parcel Service (UPS), American Express, Avon Products, Marriott International, Caterpillar Inc., and the General Electric Company.

Since the mid-1980s authors Ron Zemke, Karl Albrecht, Philip Crosby, Tom Peters, Ken Baldwin, and many others have taken up the sword of American quality prophet Peter Demming; they have written articles and books, lectured and "seminared" the business world of America. The search has been on for the magic thumb that could plug the bursting dike of dissatisfaction being proclaimed by each company's customers, both U.S. domestic and international, at the quality of American products and services. At the same time Swiss, German, English, French, and Japanese companies were selling their products faster than American customers could buy them.

Success in the United States has historically been measured by a company's ability to meet its quarterly financial objectives, often regardless of the cost to customer relations.

American business has held itself accountable to the big four of productivity, sales, profit, and return on investment. The general feeling of many American businesses in the years following the Second World War was that if a customer fell to a competitor...there was always another customer out there to take the first one's place. For a time that may have been true. In the population boom of the 1940s and 1950s, when the U.S. dollar earned had a value far greater than it has in the

1990s consumer spending in the United States reached an all-time high. The generation that had survived the Depression found the affluence of the 1950s and 1960s heady going. Businesses couldn't keep up with the demands to supply both American consumers and the recovering postwar economies of European and Pacific Rim countries. From manufacturing to financial services to housing, American businesses created themselves to meet the ever increasing demands for product and service.

In this massive movement to supply demand, the vital component for long term, successful business, *quality*, was sacrificed to the god of profit. There were some, however, who heeded another voice; knowing that history teaches tomorrow's lessons, they looked to past successes to find their futures. Service oriented businesses such as L. L. Bean, McDonald's Corporation, and Holiday Inns of America perceived that quality products and services would not only draw the original customers but keep them coming back. Senior officers of these companies had only to look at the international business headliners to find a basis for operational standards and procedures. Rolex, Porsche, Rolls-Royce, Chanel, and The Ritz Carlton, among others, offered products and services priced for the top of the consumer market. Customers lined up to pay unheard of prices for watches, automobiles, clothes, jewelry, perfume, and hospitality.

Three American businessmen, Leon Leonwood Bean, Ray Kroc, and Kemmett Wilson, understood the key concepts for success that these international service and retail giants were putting into practice:

Key Concepts for Success

- Give the customers products and services that are produced with quality product.

- Give the customers quality products and services that match the customer's perceived value of those products/services.

- Give the customers what they want. This applies to new products/services as well as to service to the original product/service, returns without dissent, timely repair, creative response to customer requests, and so on.

■ LEON LEONWOOD BEAN

Leon Leonwood Bean, founder of the L. L. Bean Company in Freeport, Maine operated his business based on a committment to the customer. His belief was that you should, "sell good merchandise at a reasonable profit, treat your customers like human beings, and they will always come back for more" (L. L. Bean, 1997), guaranteeing 100% customer satisfaction.

The L. L. Bean Company has been outstanding at incorporating these key concepts into what has become one of the most successful direct retail marketing businesses in the United States today. Customers ordering from an L. L. Bean catalog will find that:

- All products have a value equal to or greater than the price tag. Equipment and clothing is constructed to last longer than the customer expects under reasonable conditions.

- Customer Service is at the center of all business efforts. Telephone sales personnel have experience with the catalog merchandise and are familiar with operating instructions, sizing, colors, fabrics, and so on.

- Products are developed to answer customer requests.

At L. L. Bean:

Priority # 1 is getting the product to the customer.

Priority # 2 is making sure that the customer is satisfied.

Priority # 3 is expediting returns, exchanges, and service repair.

In 1996 sales for the L. L. Bean Company reached over a billion dollars in gross sales with more than 4.5 million customers worldwide (Source: L. L. Bean Company).

■ RAY KROC

Ray Kroc purchased his first restaurant from the McDonald brothers in 1954. From the outset Ray Kroc's primary business objective was to:

- Provide quality family foodservice at an affordable price in a timely manner.

Kroc entered the marketplace at a time when the average American family was beginning to feel the need for foodservice outside of the home. Driven by the emergence of two income families where parents had less time for food preparation, this need was fueled by an increasing demand for reasonably priced food prepared outside of the home. McDonald's provided an answer to their customers' needs and gave them "Change Back from Your Dollar." McDonald's standards of operation have had, from its inception, the following objectives:

- All products will have a value equal to or greater than the price tag.

- All products will be consistent in preparation and presentation to the customer.

- A consistent quality of product will be delivered in a timely manner.

- Products will be developed to respond to customer needs (Source: McDonald's Corporation).

McDonald's clearly identified its level in the hamburger marketplace. McDonald's supplies a 1/4 lb. hamburger using

USDA inspected meats with a roll, garnish, and condiments for a price that meets the customers' needs. The level of food quality is equal to the price tag.

McDonald's counter service personnel are familiar with all products and should have the ability to explain product content and varieties to customers.

At McDonald's:

Priority #1 is delivering a consistent quality of product to the customer in a timely manner.

Priority #2 is making sure that the customer is satisfied with the product.

Priority #3 is expediting returns and exchanges.

The primary goal is to create a return customer, time after time after time. By 1997 McDonald's Corporation and its franchisees operated 21,000 restaurants in over 100 countries internationally.

The focus on quality at McDonald's Corporation is established through its mandatory food specification and distribution policies to owners and franchisees. An early advertising slogan for McDonald's was "You Deserve a Break Today...At McDonald's." "We're Here for You" was the mid-1990s customer service quality statement.

McDonald's advertising efforts are focused, not simply on selling hamburgers, but on making customers "feel good" about the company's products and services.

■ KEMMONS WILSON

Kemmons Wilson developed the concept of Holiday Inns to fill a customer need in the lodging industry for accommodations offering a clean, pleasantly decorated hotel room at a price below full service hotels but above that of small independent motels. Holiday Inn motels offered limited service hotel facilities, such as restaurants, with the convenience of "drive up to the room" parking. Rooms were designed to offer comfortable but not luxurious accommodations, and were priced accordingly. To further meet customer needs, a central reservation system was put into practice, allowing Holiday Inn's customers the conveniences of making all of their overnight reservations for a trip at the same time and of changing those reservations whenever necessary. Holiday Inn's reservation system guaranteed their customers:

- A consistent quality standard of hotel accommodation at the end of a day's travel...guaranteed.

- A guaranteed room rate that matched or exceeded the perceived value of the accommodations.

- Customer service policies that expedited room rate adjustments, complaints, and refunds.

When Holiday Inns of America became Holiday Inns International it was the single largest hotel company in the world.

The primary objective of "Holiday Inns of America" was to:

- Deliver a consistent quality product at a price perceived by the customer as fair and reasonable.

At Holiday Inns of America:

> Priority #1 is consistent quality product available in a timely manner.

> Priority #2 is making sure that the customer is satisfied with the product.

> Priority #3 is expediting service requests and complaints.

The story of success repeats itself, not only in these three company profiles, but in hundreds of thousands of successful businesses across America. There is no secret to their success...only the reality that matching the customers' expectations with a consistent quality product and/or service leads to success. Whether the product is a canoe, a hamburger, or a hotel room, customers continue to patronize businesses because they are guaranteed a quality of product and service that can be relied upon over and over again. Customers also know, on the rare occasion when a product or service is not up to expectations, that their needs will be met, the problem will be rectified, and the product replaced or proper restitution made. All three of these companies practice the Keys to Service Success and, by doing so, *guarantee quality service...any time...every time.*

2

THE KEYS
TO SUCCESS

I n the increasingly competitive market of the 1990s, companies of every type have tried to reinvent the *customer service wheel*, often discussed by Karl Albrecht in his books: *The Only Thing That Matters* and *Service America*. Most owners and operators fail to realize that the *keys to success* were discovered long ago and only need to be applied to the business marketplace of the 21st century. As practiced by L. L. Bean, McDonald's, Holiday Inns, and a host of other American and international companies, the keys are as shown in Figure 2-1.

In the hectic business atmosphere of food and beverage operations, owners and managers constantly ask for a way to solve customer service problems. "Somewhere," they say over and over, "there has to be an answer to stopping customer complaints, increasing table turnovers, and increasing revenues." The answer they seek is in the statement: Increased table turnovers and revenues will happen automatically if all efforts are focused on eliminating customer complaints. To put it more simply, the answer is to *create satisfied customers*.

Give the customers quality product.

Match or exceed the customers' perceived value of products and services.

Give the customers what they want and what they need.

FIGURE 2-1
Keys to success

Goals, objectives, priorities—these three words appear in almost every discussion of management practices. Creating a "mission statement" for your business, identifying overall company goals, establishing objectives to be reached, prioritizing objectives, and establishing time lines to reach them, these are all part of every good business plan.

An admirable mission statement for a foodservice operation might be, for example:

> To provide quality food and service to the general public in a safe and healthy environment.

Overall company goals will, of course, include reaching established revenue and profit goals. Objectives within these goals will include issues such as labor turnover, table occupancy rates, control of operating costs, and others.

Where, however, in all of this is the most important component to the success of any business: the customer? Regardless of mission statements, company goals, or objectives, *the number one priority—the one to which more attention should be paid than to anything else—is **the customer**.*

If planning and production efforts are directed at *satisfying the customer, then success in every other aspect of your business will follow:*

Results of Customer Satisfaction

- Increased revenues
- Increased guest satisfaction levels
- Long-term employee relationships

- Increased profits

- Personal satisfaction

When the attention of owners and managers is focused on any issue other than the customer, business efforts will not be as successful as they could be.

If you were to ask most foodservice owners and operators to list the most important element to their success, many would say location, others food quality, some atmosphere...only a few would put the customer at the top of the list.

When we focus on the customer as the most important element, it becomes easy to identify and prioritize the other elements of a foodservice business. Figure 2-2 shows the customer in the proper place: at the center of the service wheel.

Other elements high on the priority list of a foodservice operation can now be arranged as spokes in a wheel radiating from the hub that represents the customer. All planning is done with the customer as the primary focus, not with the owner as the center of interest.

The six primary elements that affect the operation of a foodservice business, as indicated in Figure 2-3, are:

- Location

- Theme/concept

- Quality of food

- Quality of service

- Pricing

- Service style

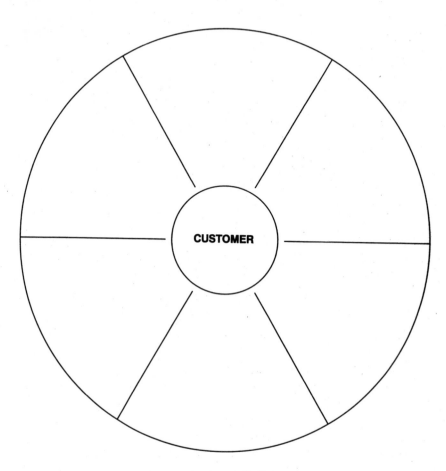

FIGURE 2-2
Service wheel A

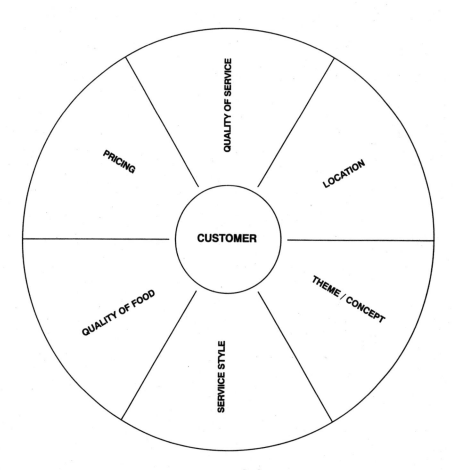

FIGURE 2-3
Service wheel B

THE QUALITY SERVICE CUSTOMER

EVALUATING CURRENT CONDITIONS

HOW TO: The objective of this section is to determine how close your business is to meeting your customer's needs and expectations.

With the service wheel in hand and the customer firmly planted in the center, use this tool to evaluate your present business. Try the following service wheel evaluation exercise.

Ask your ownership committee the following questions:

1. The restaurant is in its present location because:

   _____

   _____

   EXAMPLE: We thought that this was the best real estate buy in the area.

2. The theme/concept of the operation is

   _____

   because:_____

   _____

   EXAMPLE: I had always wanted a sports bar.

3. The quality level of the food and beverage products is:

   _____

   because:_____

   _____

EXAMPLE: Fair because we don't really know much about food and we don't get many complaints.

4. Menu prices are determined according to:

_____

EXAMPLE: We take the competition's price and mark it up or make the price what we think the item should sell for.

5. The level of service was determined by:

_____

_____

EXAMPLE: We wanted to have a formal atmosphere for the restaurant.

Count up the number of times "I" or "We" appears in the responses, then count up the number of times "customer" or "guest" appears.

I/We _____   Customer/Guest _____

Whose needs are really being addressed by current operations practices: owners or customers? If all of the responses are in the customer column, then congratulations—you are already on the way to Total Quality Service. If, however, there are responses in the "I/we" column...there's work to be done.

■ KEEPING UP WITH YOUR CUSTOMERS

Just when you think that you have all your customers fitting neatly into round holes on your customer service board...they go and change on you. Often the change is slow, barely perceptible...and usually it is the observant operator, stopping to watch the passing flow, who catches up with the customer before the complete change has taken place. The "too busy to stop" operators will still be trying to sell shots and beer when their young single customers have become families patronizing pizza restaurants that cater to children and offer beer and wine.

Retail operators in the beach resort of Rehoboth, Delaware, found just such a change during a recent summer. The most observant among them such as Dominick Pulieri, owner of Grotto Restaurants Inc., however, had been watching national restaurant trends and began offering a concept restaurant such as The Grand Slam, shown in Figure 3-1, to families of all ages.

Continually evaluating customers and identifying their changing needs is an often overlooked function of owners and managers. The most practical way to keep ahead of the changing picture is to be at the door, greeting customers on a day-to-day basis and taking note of changing needs and profiles. Operators need to welcome new products, promotions, and ideas from staff, customers, and vendors. Owners and managers need to be ready when, or before, the customer is. When businesses change with the customer, they are much closer to achieving Total Quality Service.

With each change of season, stores are expected to present their customers with the newest fashions, preferably ahead of the competition. One of the most recent arrivals on the U.S. scene, one of the newest movers and shakers, is IKEA, a Swedish retail furniture and accessory company. IKEA has been carefully selecting store sites in the United States that will provide local customers for 200,000 square feet of display and stock retail space. IKEA is hugely successful, with over $480 million in sales internationally, due to the practice of some revolutionary theories in customer service. In a Harvard Business Review article, futurist Alvin Toffler discusses IKEA's method, calling it "the value-creating system" with the customer at the center as a "prosumer."

IKEA wants its customers to understand that their role is not to consume value, but to create it. In this new logic of value, companies do not really compete with one another. Rather it is the offerings that compete for the time and attention and money of the customer. A company must create dialogue with its customers in order to repeat the performance over and over again and keep its offerings competitive. (HBR, August 1993.)

This "dialogue" is established through customer surveys, such as the one seen in Figure 4-2, and through focus groups, a practice not unknown to American foodservice companies. IKEA wants to know what its customers want and don't want to buy. Once customer needs and wants are identified, the company goes to work satisfying them.

IKEA regularly surveys the communities surrounding its stores, up to a distance of 40 to 60 miles, and has identified four levels of customers:

FIGURE 3-1
Grotto Pizza Grand Slam Restaurant

- Have visited the store and love it

- Have visited but are unsure if they will return

- Have not yet visited the store

- Have no intention of shopping at IKEA (Focus, March 1995)

IKEA's surveys are more than customer comment forms. They are a series of probing questions that solicit a broad range of information on current and potential customers.

Applying IKEA's concept of having the customer determine

product value offerings to a foodservice operation requires reorganizing the customer survey process. Many foodservice operations offer customer cards such as those pictured in Figures 3-2 and 3-3. Both surveys ask the customer to react to specific surface issues as well as provide information on reason for visit, frequency of visits, and possibility of return. Figure 3-3 surveys customers in more detail, asking questions designed to elicit product development and service reactions from the company. Figure 3-4, by comparison, asks the customer to take as little effort as possible to document their opinions. Unfortunately this brief a comment card does not guide the customer to provide specific information and can result in inconclusive survey results. Foodservice operators who would like to emulate IKEA's success should develop surveys such as Figures 3-2 and 3-3.

"The customer will never take the time to fill this out!" This is a common reaction to this type of survey technique, and one that has merit. The answer is *give them a reason* to do so. Coupons and discounts for returning the survey, sweepstake offers, prizes, all "create a value" to customers for taking the time to *give you their information.* U.S. Air recently offered a 500 mile credit to customers' frequent flyer accounts for completing and returning a survey: good value for their time and information.

What makes a Bennigans' Restaurant or a TGI Friday's any less of a retail outlet than a Bullock's, a Macy's, or even an IKEA? Apply successful marketing strategies to your operation.

Trends are evident in the continual appearance of steakhouse restaurants in the American marketplace of the 1990s.

Lonestar, Longhorn, Outback, and Houston's are just four national brand restaurant groups competing with independents in most of the significant communities in the United States. Capitalizing on the popularity of casual dining, country music, and a revived interest in eating beef, these restaurants compete among themselves for the portion of the consumer market that wants a casual, relaxed steakhouse atmosphere for a foodservice experience. The marketing tactics that they apply to compete among themselves for market share serve as an important example of how to evaluate the target market customer.

EL TOVAR

	Which meal did you have?	☐ Breakfast
		☐ Lunch
		☐ Dinner

TO OUR GUESTS
Using the rating system below, please help us evaluate our services by answering these questions.
4 - Excellent, 3 - Good, 2 - Fair, 1 - Poor

Date:_____

Server's Name: _____
If you met an outstanding employee, please let us know his or her name.

_____

HOSPITALITY
Did you feel welcome?   [ ]

YOUR ADDITIONAL COMMENTS AND SUGGESTIONS

Was the Host polite and courteous?   [ ]

Were you thanked & invited to return?   [ ]

RESTAURANT APPEARANCE
Did our staff have a neat, clean appearance?   [ ]

Was the restaurant clean overall?   [ ]

OPTIONAL

FOOD AND SERVICE
Was food served promptly?   [ ]
Was your order correct?   [ ]
Was your food properly prepared?   [ ]
Was hot food served HOT?   [ ]
Did you receive courteous service?   [ ]

NAME

_____

ADDRESS

_____

CITY   STATE   ZIP

(Upon completion, either give to cashier or mail.)

AN d**Amfac** RESORT

FIGURE 3-2
El Tovar comment card

1. **Your age:**
   □ 18-24   □ 35-44   □ 55-64
   □ 25-34   □ 45-54   □ 65+

2. **Your sex:**   □ Male   □ Female

3. **Your Zip Code:** __ __ __ __ __

4. **How often do you eat here?**
   □ < 1x/month   □ 2x-4x/month
   □ 1x-2x/month   □ 5x+/month

5. **What prompted your visit today?**
   □ Special occasion   □ Entertaining clients
   □ Advertising   □ Felt like eating out
   □ Other: _____

6. **Were you promptly and warmly greeted by our staff?**
   □ Yes   □ No

7. **My server today was (check all that apply)**
   □ Friendly   □ Courteous   □ Rude
   □ Polite   □ Impolite   □ Cheerful
   □ Preoccupied   □ Knowledgeable   □ Efficient
   □ Helpful   □ Fun   □ Slow

8. **How would you rate your service today?**
   □ Excellent   □ Good   □ Fair   □ Poor

9. **How would you rate our quality and selection of food?**
   □ Excellent   □ Good   □ Fair   □ Poor

10. **How would you rate our variety and selection of beer?**
    □ Excellent   □ Good   □ Fair   □ Poor

11. **How do you rate the overall value of our products and services?**
    □ Excellent   □ Good   □ Fair   □ Poor

12. **How would you rate our cleanliness—in the bar, dining room, and rest rooms?**
    □ Excellent   □ Good   □ Fair   □ Poor

13. **What type of live music would you like to listen to at Iron Hill? (check all that apply)**
    □ Jazz/R & B   □ Folk/Acoustic
    □ Pop/Rock   □ No opinion
    □ Irish   □ No live music
    □ Blues   □ Other: _____

14. **Would you recommend us to others?**
    □ Yes, I would highly recommend Iron Hill
    □ I may recommend Iron Hill
    □ I would not recommend Iron Hill to anyone

Additional Comments: _____

FIGURE 3-3
Ironhill comment card

Lonestar Restaurants recreate the atmosphere of an American Western bar and restaurant: rustic wood, long tables, waitresses in short pants with western design shirts, country music, peanut shells on the floor, and very casual service are the setting for the application of the keys to success shown in Figure 3-5. Food quality is consistently high, service is casual and friendly, music is loud, and raucous behavior is not discouraged.

Longhorn Restaurants takes a similar theme and dresses it up with colorful accessories and menu variety, as seen in Figures 3-6 and 3-7.

What will you tell your friends about Einsteins?

We want to know anything you like or don't like about Einstein Bros™ Bagels, and any suggestions you have for improving our food, service or atmosphere. Got some great idea? We'd like to know. Got a gripe? We definitely need to know if you've got a compliment; we'd love to hear it, too. Just fill this card out and give it to one of our employees or managers. Thank you.

_____

_____

_____

_____

_____

_____

_____

_____

(Fill this out if you want)

Submitted by: _____

Name: _____

Address: _____

Phone: _____

FIGURE 3-4

Einstein's comment card

Outback Restaurants highlight an Australian theme in a rustic setting. Accessories that reference Australia, a selection of Australian beers, and menu copy incorporating Australian slang phrases provide a slightly different atmosphere from the American Western theme. Service is casual, food quality is consistent, and there is little to distinguish this concept from any other. What makes their customers keep coming back? *The total quality customer experience.*

Houston's Restaurants, pictured in Figure 3-8, offers a more upscale steakhouse in a contemporary setting with a limited menu. Service is fast, accurate, and professional. The quality of food is good and the overall experience consistently pleasant. The key to Houston's success is a quality service training program and the application of the keys to success seen in Figure 3-5.

Chicken rotisserie theme restaurants are another of the latest trends in concept food operations to hit the American marketplace. Currently rolling out new concepts are Boston Market and Kenny Rogers Roasters. Both chains offer rotisserie chicken in a self-service, quick food format specializing

 Give the customers quality product.

 Match or exceed the customers' perceived value of products and services.

 Give the customers what they want and what they need.

FIGURE 3-5

Keys to success

FIGURE 3-6
Interior of a Longhorn Restaurant

in home replacement meals with menu offerings that are almost identical. The differences that distinguish the two concepts are the taste of their chicken coating, the atmosphere in which they serve it, and the quality of the total customer experience. Many locations, for both chains, are former Roy Rogers Restaurants or similar fast-food chicken operators. Boston

FIGURE 3-7
Longhorn Menu

STARTERS

Tongue-tingling starters guaranteed to spur your appetite!

Texas Cheese Fries
Seasoned french fries loaded with Texas Chili, three kinds of cheese, bacon and jalapeños. $4.95

Prairie Peppers
Mild jalapeños stuffed with three cheeses and served with a special dipping sauce. $4.95

Baby Back Ribs
Half-rack, tender and tangy. Served with barbeque sauce. $6.95

Grilled Shrimp
Seasoned shrimp, chargrilled and served with cocktail sauce and a lemon wedge. $6.95

Chicken Fingers
Chicken tenders lightly breaded and fried. Served with honey-mustard. $4.25

Crispy Shrimp
Shrimp lightly breaded and fried. Served with cocktail sauce. $5.95

Soup of the Day
Hearty soup, made fresh daily.
cup $1.95   bowl $2.75

Authentic Texas Chili
No beans about it! Our authentic recipe topped with onions and cheese with a jalapeño on the side.
cup $2.25   bowl $3.25

Tomato and Onion Salad
Shaved red onions, layered between slices of our vine-ripe tomatoes. Topped with crumbled bleu cheese and vinaigrette dressing. $2.95

FRESH CHICKEN

A bounty of Longhorn chicken favorites. All feature an 8 oz. top-quality boneless, skinless breast guaranteed to be tender and tasty.

Longhorn Rocky Top Chicken
Chicken smothered with cheddar and Monterey Jack cheese, BBQ sauce, bacon, diced tomatoes and green onions. Served with Double-Jack Beans™ and french fries. $8.95

Charbroiled Chicken
Absolutely the juiciest, tenderest chicken breast you'll find. Served with rice and Garden-Patch Vegetables. Also available with our spicy Cajun seasonings. $7.95

BBQ Chicken
Basted with our special sauce and charbroiled to perfection. Served with Double-Jack Beans™ and french fries. $7.95

Chicken K-Bob
Grilled chicken breast with onions, green peppers, mushrooms and tomatoes. Served with rice and Garden-Patch Vegetables. $7.95

All chicken dinners are served with hearth-baked bread and the perfect side dishes listed above. Add a Mixed Green or Caesar Salad for only $1.95.

LEGENDARY STEAKS

Longhorn Legends since 1981. We own our own meat company to ensure your steak is absolutely the best quality we can serve. Our steaks are always fresh (never frozen) and hand-cut from USDA Choice, Midwestern corn-fed beef. We pride ourselves on cooking them up just the way you like it, too!
Rare – red, cool center; Medium Rare – warm red center; Medium – warm and pink throughout; Medium Well – very warm throughout, pink almost gone; Well – very warm and brown throughout.

Flo's Filet
Our most popular choice, cut fresh from the tenderloin.
9 oz. $13.95   7 oz. $12.45

Beef K-Bob
Filet cuts grilled with onions, green peppers, mushrooms and tomatoes. 6 oz. $9.95

Ribeye
The choice of the Legendary Texas Rangers. Tender and juicy, cut from the rib loin. 12 oz. $13.95

The Renegade
A hearty top sirloin steak, sprinkled with Prairie Dust™, our own special blend of zesty seasonings. 12 oz. $11.95

N.Y. Strip
The steak lover's choice, with a robust steak flavor you can sink your teeth into.
14 oz. $15.95   11oz. $13.95

Chop Steak
Ground sirloin, smothered with onions and mushrooms. 10 oz. $7.95

Texas T-Bone
Flavorful and distinctive, includes a Filet and a N.Y. Strip. 16 oz. $15.95

The Longhorn
Our special, giant Porterhouse cut actually includes a filet and a NY strip in one, delicious cut. 22 oz. $17.95

Our legendary steaks are served with a Mixed Green or Caesar salad, hearth-baked bread, and choice of potato, rice or vegetables.

COMBO CORRAL

Round up your favorite entrees and lasso them together for a combo sure to please any appetite!

Salmon & Filet
7 oz. fresh-cut Canadian King salmon and 7 oz. fresh tenderloin Filet served with a loaded baked potato. $17.95

Grilled Shrimp & Filet
Chargrilled shrimp and 7 oz. fresh tenderloin Filet served with rice and Garden-Patch Vegetables. $17.95

Baby Back Ribs & BBQ Chicken
Tender baby back ribs and basted, charbroiled BBQ chicken served with Double-Jack Beans™ and french fries. $13.95

All combo dinners are served with the perfect side dishes listed above, a Mixed Green or Caesar salad, and our hearth-baked bread.

F I G U R E 3-7 (continued)

FIGURE 3-8
Houston's Restaurant exterior. Pompano Beach, Florida.

Market, Figure 3-9, offers a bright, colorful decor with friend-ly, smiling, and helpful counter staff. Kenny Rogers Roasters, Figure 3-10, offers Kenny Rogers. Entertainment is the theme with television monitors placed for easy viewing of Kenny Rogers music videos from all restaurant locations. Service is "down-home country" friendly. Both concepts offer value-added service: Kenny Rogers...entertainment, Boston Market...one-stop shopping

MENU

THE FOOD'S ALWAYS BETTER AT THE MARKET™

BOSTON
Home Style Meals
MARKET

FIGURE 3-9
Boston Market Menu

INDIVIDUAL MEALS

ROTISSERIE CHICKEN
With 2 Sides & Combread

1/4 Dark (Leg & Thigh)	4.49
1/4 White (Breast & Wing)	5.49
*Half Chicken	6.49

* Additional charge for all white meat

KID'S MEALS 10 and Under
All include Kid's size side, combread & drink

Mac & Cheese	1.99
Kid's size serving of Chicken, Turkey, Ham or Meat Loaf	2.49

ROTISSERIE TURKEY
With 2 Sides & Combread

Carved Turkey Breast	5.99

BOSTON HEARTH™ HAM
With 2 Sides & Combread

Carved Ham	5.99

DOUBLE SAUCED MEAT LOAF
With 2 Sides & Combread

Carved Meat Loaf	5.49

CHICKEN POT PIE
With 1 Side & Combread

Pot Pie with Combread	5.49
	4.49

FAMILY MEALS

FEAST #1 Serves 2-3	FAMILY FEAST #2 Serves 3-4	BIG FEAST #3 Serves 4-5	DOUBLE FEAST #4 Serves 5-6
1 Chicken* or 1 Meat Loaf 2 Large Sides 3 Cornbreads **13.99**	1 Chicken* or 1 Meat Loaf 3 Large Sides 4 Cornbreads **16.99**	1 1/2 Chickens* or 1 1/2 Meat Loaves 4 Large Sides 5 Cornbreads **20.99**	2 Chickens* or 2 Meat Loaves 5 Large Sides 6 Cornbreads **24.99**
4 Servings of Turkey or Ham 2 Large Sides 3 Cornbreads **15.99**	4 Servings of Turkey or Ham 3 Large Sides 4 Cornbreads **18.99**	6 Servings of Turkey or Ham 4 Large Sides 5 Cornbreads **23.99**	8 Servings of Turkey or Ham 5 Large Sides 6 Cornbreads **27.99**

* Additional Charge for All White Meat

BOSTON CARVER® SANDWICHES

Choice of French White or Honey Wheat Bread
with Lettuce & Tomato

	Sandwich	Combo*
CHICKEN CARVER® with Cheddar Cheese & Creamy Dijon	4.49	5.49
TURKEY CARVER® with Swiss Cheese & Creamy Parmesan	4.49	5.49
MEAT LOAF CARVER® with Cheddar Cheese & Hickory Ketchup	4.49	5.49
CARVER® CLUB with Ham, Turkey, Swiss, Cheddar & Club Sauce with Bacon	4.49	5.49
HAM CARVER® with Swiss Cheese & Creamy Dijon	4.49	5.49

* Combo includes Individual Side & 16 oz. Drink

SIDE ITEMS

Mashed Potatoes	Cinnamon Apples
Herbed Sweet Corn	Baked Beans
Savory Stuffing	Creamed Spinach
Steamed Vegetables	Cole Slaw
Garlic Dill New Potatoes	Caesar Salad
Macaroni & Cheese	Cranberry Walnut Relish

Ask about our Seasonal Sides

Individual 1.59 • Large 3.49

SIDE ITEM SAMPLER
Choice of any 3 sides with cornbread 4.49

Prices May Vary By Location

PM-24 8/97

EVERYTHING ELSE

SOUPS

	Individual	Large
Hearty Chicken	1.59	3.49

SALADS Served with cornbread

Chicken Caesar Salad	
Caesar Salad	4.49
Chunky Chicken Salad with 2 Sides	3.29
	5.49

SWEETS

Freshly Baked Brownies & Cookies	.99 ea.

DRINKS

Small	.99	Regular	1.19
Coffee	.99		

FIGURE 3-10
Kenny Rogers Roasters Menu

CAPTURING
MARKET SHARE

C apturing your market share of customers requires that you review and evaluate *customer priority issues*. The objective of studying customer priority issues is to discover information about the customer not already known or available which will be used to determine what the customer really wants a food-service operation to look like, taste like, feel like, and cost. This information will then be applied to product development as well as to determination of pricing policies, entertainment themes, and restaurant concepts. These efforts are designed to increase the percentage of available customers patronizing your foodservice operation.

To establish customer priority issues it is necessary to identify marketing related customer information and develop customer profiles for the principal consumer groups that are serviced on a regular basis. Figure 4-1 lists some of the major areas of information that need to be identified in developing a customer profile:

- Age: _____

- Income: _____

- Family Status:_____

- Education:_____

- Occupation:_____

FIGURE 4-1
Average Customer Profile

A format that can be used as a guideline for gathering this information is seen in Figure 4-2. Add the following information to the survey results related to your customer and your restaurant:

- Travel Distance: —————————————————————
- Transportation: —————————————————————
- Motivation for patronizing restaurant:

—————————————————————————————————————

■ CUSTOMER SERVICE ISSUES

The results of market survey research may reveal two or more customer profiles as happened in the case of Sfuzzi's in downtown San Diego, California. In order to maximize the opportu-

CUSTOMER PROFILE
DEMOGRAPHIC INFORMATON

	TOTAL	(%)
Total Adults	**5,840**	**100.0**
Men	1,643	28.1
Women	4,197	71.9
Age		Median Age 43.0 Years
25-34	1,120	19.2
25-49	3,377	57.8
25-54	3,928	67.3
35-44	1,615	27.6
35-54	2,808	48.1
Education		
Grad Colege+	1,862	31.9
Att/Grad College	4,155	71.1
Employment Status		
Employed	4,267	73.1
Full-Time	3,561	61.0
Occupation		
Prof/Mgr	1,629	27.9
Household Income		Median HHI $53,572
HHI $75,000+	1,523	26.1
HHI $60,000+	2,412	41.3
HHI $50,000+	3,203	54.8
Individual Employment Income		Median IEI $27,643
IEI $50,000+	666	11.4
IEI $40,000+	1,168	20.0
IEI $30,000+	1,870	32.0
Marital Status		
Married	3,662	62.7
Single	1,193	20.4
Home Ownership		Median Home Value $136,376
Own Home	4,208	72.1
Home Value $100,000+	2,843	48.7

FIGURE 4-2
Market survey guideline

nities for increasing customer counts and revenues, it is necessary in such situations to identify customer service issues for each consumer group and determine how to meet those needs successfully.

Sfuzzi's realized that their location in the downtown business area generated three customer groups related to business:

- Business lunch group
- Singles happy hour group
- Business dinner group

Sfuzzi's downtown location is also in the heart of the tourist/convention area, which generates two additional customer groups:

- Tourist/convention lunch group
- Tourist/convention dinner group

Downtown San Diego's waterfront has developed large numbers of condominiums and is easily accessed by the suburban communities. A large retirement age population group lives in both the city and the surrounding suburbs, which generates an additional customer group:

- Senior citizen dinner group

Affluent San Diego residents are interested in restaurants as an atmosphere for social occasions, creating yet another customer group:

- Social diners group

In all, Sfuzzi's has identified six customer groups and their respective customer service issues as they apply to the restaurant location in downtown San Diego; these are outlined in Figure 4-3.

Customer Group	Service Issue
Business Group	Fast lunch service
	Casual/upscale dinner service
Singles Group	Upscale bar service between 4 PM and 7 PM
	Late night food availability
Convention Group	Fast lunch service
	Casual/upscale dinner service
	Late night food availability
Tourist Group	Casual/upscale dinner service
	Late night food availability
Senior Group	Discounted dinner prices
	Casual/upscale dinner service
	Convenient/safe parking
Social Group	Casual/upscale dinner service
	Late night food availability
	Well developed wine list
	Italian cuisine experience

FIGURE 4-3

Customer groups and service issues: Sfuzzi's, San Diego, California.

FIGURE 4-4
Sfuzzi's San Diego Restaurant Interior.

To take full advantage of all these potential customer groups, Sfuzzi's San Diego has:

- Designed an Italian Bistro restaurant concept: interior design is light, interesting, and sophisticated, as shown in Figure 4-4.

- Developed a level of service that is upscale casual.

- Committed to serving high quality food items.

- Developed a range of menu items to include Italian cuisine items as well as regional American seafood.

- Created an extensive wine list.

- Provided valet parking.

- Developed a menu program that includes:

    Early bird menu discounts for seniors

    Express lunch for business/convention customers

    Discount happy hour for singles

    Full à la carte dinner menu for social/business/tourist/convention groups

    Late night snacks for social/tourist convention groups

    Monthly seven course wine dinner for social group

Sfuzzi's management theory for the San Diego location is that the "service needs" of all the customer groups in their marketplace must be met if revenue goals are to be reached. Meeting customer service needs is a priority for the Sfuzzi's Restaurant Group, and their bottom line shows it.

■ IDENTIFYING CUSTOMER SERVICE ISSUES

HOW TO: The objective of this segment is to apply the suggested survey and information analysis guidelines to identify your customers' needs and issues.

Using the market survey guideline in Figure 4-2, identify the five customer profile areas of information listed in Figure 4-1 (average customer profile).

Average Customer Profile

■ Age: _____

■ Income: _____

■ Family Status: _____

■ Education: _____

■ Occupation: _____

■ Travel distance: _____

■ Transportation: _____

■ Motivation for patronizing restaurant: _____

_____

List the most commonly noted motivations for patronizing your restaurant and assign age groups to each motivation:

Age Groups: 20-30

30-45

45-65

Motivation   Age

_____   _____

_____   _____

_____   _____

_____   _____

What does the average customer need? Possibilities include: affordable menu prices; accommodations for children; accessible transportation or parking; a foodservice operation within 15 minutes of home or office; an entertainment theme that provides activity and/or atmosphere as well as food and beverages.

Using the outline in Figure 4-5, identify customer service issues for each motivation. What do *your* customers need to find when they come to *your* restaurant?

Are the customer service issues that have been listed currently available in your operation? If not, use this exercise as a good starting point for reorganizing your business to provide Total Quality Customer Service.

Motivation   **Customer Service Issue**
(Customer Group)

FIGURE 4-5
Customer Service Issues by motivation

THE SUCCESSFUL
SERVICE EXPERIENCE

Now that you have the customers....what are you going to do with them?

■ CREATE SATISFIED CUSTOMERS

The president of a small chain of family restaurants recently related this story with a look of bemused confusion. He had provided the important elements for a successful service experience for his customer and it still went wrong.

Elements for Successful Customer Service Experience

- Quality food
- Quality service
- Pleasant atmosphere
- Value for price paid

His story begins in a meeting with an irate customer. The customer had taken the time to come to the company office personally to relate the embarrassment and confusion caused by one employee failing to respond to "Customer Need." The customer, along with his wife, had entered the restaurant intending to use a promotional coupon. After presenting the server with the coupon, a meal was ordered, enjoyed, and the check presented. The customer's experience up to this point had been completely satisfactory. As the couple prepared to leave the restaurant, they presented the check and food coupon to the cashier, who promptly refused to accept the coupon, claiming that it could not be applied to the food items that had been ordered during the time period in which they had been served. Although the customer explained that the server had accepted the promotional coupon, the cashier remained firm. The coupon would not be honored and the full menu price would have to be paid.

As the restaurant was busy, a line of customers was waiting to pay, and only further confusion and public embarrassment would be gained by bringing management into the picture, the couple paid as demanded and left, embarrassed, confused, and certainly unhappy with their experience. Everyone in the restaurant had done their job promptly and accurately to provide a quality foodservice experience. *It only took the actions of the last individual in the chain of service to create an unhappy customer.*

The embarrassing experience was undoubtedly told and retold to friends and neighbors. It was only because the customer felt a loyalty to the restaurant's management and recognized that this incident was not consistent with past experiences that he took the time to find the company president and relate the problem. Had it been a first or second visit, the customer would have simply never returned and continued to spread the story of bad service throughout the community. Fortunately direct contact and a sincere, outraged reaction on the part of the company president, along with a certificate for a free meal, satisfied the customer and assured the restaurant of his return patronage and good will.

What should the cashier have done, given the initial acceptance of the coupon by the server?

Total Quality Service Response: Empower the cashier to accept the coupon, to give the discount to the customer, and to report the matter to management if the server had incorrectly accepted the coupon.

Which customer service issues should have been recognized?

- Provide a total customer service experience
- Meet the customers' needs

The Cost of Customer Dissatisfaction

- The incalculable dollar cost of bad publicity in the community
- The dollar cost of supplying *two free meals* to replace a *$1 per meal discount* on the original coupon
- The eroding of the customer's confidence in the ability of the restaurant to meet his continued needs

Needless to say, the company president was at his wit's end about how to stop customer service problems such as this from happening again. As he said: "We tell them...over and over...the cashier should have known to accept the coupon!" *Sound familiar?*

The answer to customer service problems is to provide the staff with:

- A clear and established standard of service appropriate to the foodservice operation.
- A clearly outlined series of service steps that must be followed consistently with every service effort

- Basic and thorough training for all of the skills required to competently carry out each foodservice job position.

- A clearly outlined series of quality service points that, when added to the service steps on a consistent basis, cannot fail to provide quality service.

You too can achieve quality service!

DELIVERING
QUALITY SERVICE

In this chapter, five separate foodservice operations are offered as examples of different concepts in delivering food service to the customer:

Quick service: Counter service/self-service

Casual family style service

Casual bistro style service

Casual full-service

Formal full-service

To effectively use the illustrated service guidelines offered in this book, select the style of operation that most closely approximates your operation. Using the worksheet at the end of the appropriate section, list the critical path of service steps that would best provide quality service on a consistent basis to your customers. Identify Quality Service Points that would result in value-added service for your guests.

Before beginning these exercises, however, take a few moments to evaluate any efforts to establish quality service that are already in place within your operation. The worksheet, Evaluating Current Conditions, is a short summary to help you to identify these efforts.

WORKSHEET

EVALUATING CURRENT CONDITIONS

EXERCISE: ANSWER THE FOLLOWING QUESTIONS

Section One:
The established standard of service for this foodservice operation is (check off as appropriate to the operation's foodservice outlets):

Counter service/Self-service _____

Buffet service _____

Casual family style service _____

Casual bistro style service _____

Casual full service _____

Formal full service _____

    If there is any question as to what category your operation falls under, take the time to review the service step outlines and illustrations in the following pages. Perhaps the operation in question is a combination of styles of operation. If so, use the workpages and ideas offered here to create your own signature brand of quality service.

Section Two:
Service steps are posted for every meal service.

    Yes _____   No _____

Foodservice job skills training is required for every position.

Yes _____ No _____

"Quality Service Points" are assigned to service steps as appropriate?

Yes _____ No _____

If the answer is "no" to any or all of these three questions, compare the service steps and Quality Service Points for your operation with those offered in the following pages to see what changes can be made to improve your current service specifications.

The following chapter of this book offers five separate foodservice operations as examples of a variety of service styles. Each operation is accompanied by an illustrated "Critical Path of Service." Each critical path of service incorporates Quality Service Points as appropriate to the type of foodservice operation.

CREATING
QUALITY SERVICE

Guaranteeing quality service to both your customers and your staff requires identifying the level of service appropriate for your operation. If this has not already been established, complete the exercises outlined in the first part of this book. By determining concept, atmosphere, menu items, and level of food quality, you will establish the necessary criteria around which to develop a critical path for service staff to carry out. It is also important to assess objectively the ability of your current or prospective service employees to perform varying skill levels of table service. For example, if you are operating in a college town and most of your service staff will be hired from the available student population, then you should not expect them to perform fine points of classical table service. It would be more appropriate to plan a version of casual style table service where personality will be as important as ability to consistently perform service. If, on the other hand, you are adjacent to a large city with a population of professional servers to draw from, a full service restaurant offering a critical path of service that includes fine points of table service would be feasible.

■ CRITICAL PATH OF SERVICE

A Critical Path of Service is a list of the service steps necessary to provide consistent quality service to a customer, in the order in which they need to be performed. The critical path of service should include those activities of service that are a trademark of the operation and/or that distinguish you from the competition. For example, if the service policy is to have a greeter open the front door for customers before they approach the host or hostess, then this is the first step on the critical path of service. Anthony Athenas, in his restaurant Pier 4 in Boston, Massachusetts, created the position of "Muffin Person," sending a server onto the floor with a copper heater full of popovers to be served to the table as value-added service between the salad course and the main course. This service activity is an identified step in the critical path of service for this restaurant. The anticipation of hot popovers may be the deciding factor in choosing Pier 4 as the restaurant for the evening, or may just be a well anticipated feature. Whatever the outcome, this important distinguishing service activity becomes critical to the overall service success of Pier 4.

■ CREATING A CRITICAL PATH OF SERVICE

HOW TO: The objective of this segment is to create a critical path of service appropriate to your foodservice operation.

Analyze each meal period separately. Draw up a complete list of service steps beginning with the first contact that the guest has with the staff, using the following exercises. The following outline is a listing of the basic service steps for casual or full service lunch or dinner service. Identify each service step and the appropriate service position as it is currently performed in your operation. Number each step in the order in which your staff perform it as seen in the example below. Add or delete service steps according to the policies of your operation.

EXAMPLE:

Greeting:

Host/Hostess _Step 1_

Server: _Step 2_

Menu Presentation:

Host/Hostess: _No activity_

Server: _Step 3_

■ CRITICAL PATH OF SERVICE OUTLINE

Greeting:

　　Host/Hostess: _____

　　Server: _____

Menu Presentation:

　　Host/Hostess: _____

　　Server: _____

Beverage Order:

　　Host/Hostess: _____

　　Server: _____

Menu Order:

　　Menu Explanation: _____

　　Host/Hostess: _____

　　Order: _____

　　Server: _____

Wine Order:

Wine List Presentation: _____

Server: _____

Wine Order: _____

Server: _____

Warm Bread Service:

Bus Person: _____

Server: _____

Water Service:

Bus Person: _____

Server: _____

First Course Service:

Bus Person: _____

Server: _____

Bus First Course:

  Bus Person: _____

  Server: _____

Second Course Service:

  Bus Person: _____

  Server: _____

Beverage Replenish:

  Bus Person: _____

  Server: _____

Table Check:

  Floor Manager: _____

  Service: _____

  Other: _____

Bus Second Course:

  Bus Person: _____

  Server: _____

Dessert Course Order:

Server: _____

Dessert Course Service:

Bus Person: _____

Server: _____

Coffee Service:

Bus Person: _____

Server: _____

Check Presentation:

Server: _____

Coffee Replenish:

Bus Person: _____

Server: _____

Pickup Check:

Bus Person: _____

Server: _____

Close with Customer:

Host/Hostess: _____

Server: _____

Other: _____

Using the examples of critical paths of service offered in this section, draw up a list of numbered steps of service using the following example as a guideline.

WORKSHEET

CRITICAL PATH OF SERVICE FORMAT

STEP 1: _____

STEP 2: _____

STEP 3: _____

STEP 4: _____

STEP 5: _____

STEP 6: _____

STEP 7: _____

STEP 8: _____

STEP 9: _____

STEP 10: _____

STEP 11: _____

STEP 12: _____

STEP 13: _____

STEP 14: _____

STEP 15: _____

STEP 16: _____

STEP 17: _____

STEP 18: _____

Critical Paths of Service will be reviewed in the following pages for five different styles of food service operation: quick serve; casual family style service; casual restaurant style, breakfast service; full-service restaurant, bistro style for lunch or dinner service; and full-service restaurant dinner service. These examples of current service procedures in successful foodservice operations will serve as a guideline to help you to identify service steps and procedures for your operation.

The objective of the following Critical Paths of Service is to:

1. Provide examples of established Critical Paths of Service outlines for a variety of styles of foodservice operations.

2. Provide examples of the application of Critical Paths of Service in successful foodservice operations.

Each style of foodservice operation, beginning with quick serve, will be presented in the following sequence:

1. The established Critical Path of Service outline.

2. The application of the Critical Path of Service outline.

3. The illustrated application of the Critical Path of Service.

4. A Critical Path of Service worksheet.

TQS appears on a number of the Critical Paths of Service. This identifies your opportunity to present the customer with a *Total Quality Service* experience by providing a service, product, or activity that represents value-added service. As discussed earlier, value added service is a service experience that represents more than the customer expects for a particular menu item or service.

Five individual foodservice operations, ranging from quick service-counter service to full-service dining, provide the settings for the application of Critical Paths of Service in this section. Each operational style is successful in providing a consistent standard quality of service for both customers and owners.

Two of these examples represent national restaurant companies that offer outlets in major metropolitan areas around the United States. *Au Bon Pain* is a chain of quick service coffee and sandwich/salad kiosks and restaurants located in airports, shopping mall food courts, and freestanding locations. *Ruth Chris' Steak Houses* are full-service restaurants, located in major cities, offering lunch and dinner. Customers know what level and quality of service experiences to expect regardless of the city or location.

Grotto Restaurants Inc. is a chain of over 30 units in the State of Delaware. Like Au Bon Pain, Grotto Restaurants outlets range in format from quick-serve counters to sit-down restaurants and sports bars.

The Garden Room is a full-service hotel coffee shop serving three meals a day and open from 6:30 AM to 11:00 PM, located in the Manhattan Beach Radisson Hotel near Los Angeles International Airport.

The Reunion Inn & Grill is an independent, full-service bistro concept restaurant located in Camden, Maine. The owners have combined a six room inn and a restaurant in a converted mill building located in the center of a seaside resort community.

Au Bon Pain restaurant interior

CRITICAL PATH OF SERVICE OUTLINE
QUICK FOOD STYLE RESTAURANT—
SELF-SERVICE/COUNTER SERVICE

STEP 1:   Guest is acknowledged.

           TQS _____

STEP 2:   Host/Hostess greets guest.

STEP 3:   Counter server greets guest.

STEP 4:   Counter server presents menu and takes order.

STEP 5:   Counter server fills order.

           TQS _____

STEP 6:   Counter server checks order with guest.

STEP 7:   Counter server completes guest check transaction.

STEP 8:   Self-service is used for condiments and tableware.

STEP 9:   Self-service is used for seating.

STEP 10:   Server checks table.

           TQS _____

STEP 11: Counter server takes dessert and beverage order.

STEP 12: Counter server fills order.

TQS ————————————————————————

STEP 13: Counter server completes guest check transaction.

STEP 14: Self-service is used for condiments and tableware.

STEP 15: Self-service is used for seating.

STEP 16: Floor manager closes with guest.

Au Bon Pain offers an example of the development in the quick food style of foodservice operation. In answer to customer needs for quality baked goods and premium coffees in a self-serve/take-out setting, the Au Bon Pain Company was established in Boston, Massachusetts. The coffee-bakery concept soon evolved to include sandwiches, salads, soups, stews, and limited main course items such as grilled chicken breast and chicken pot pie.

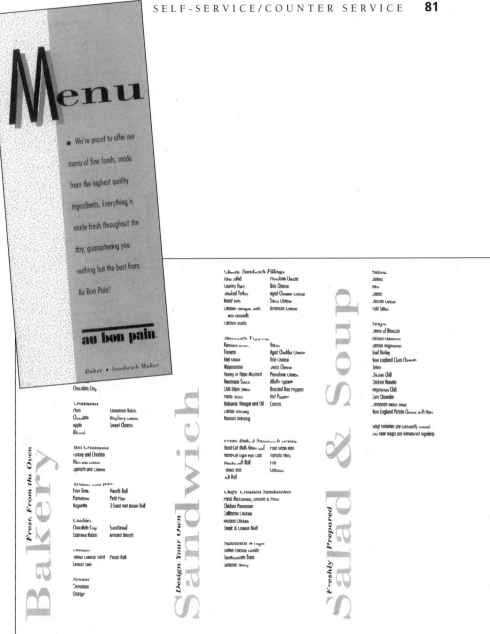

Au Bon Pain Menu

Au Bon Pain also offers an extensive catering menu to extend their customer market.

Au Bon Pain Catering Menu

AU BON PAIN RESTAURANT'S APPLICATION OF CRITICAL PATH OF SERVICE OUTLINE FOR QUICK FOOD STYLE RESTAURANT— SELF-SERVICE/COUNTER SERVICE

STEP 1:   Guest is acknowledged.

TQS: Within 1 minute.

STEP 2:   Host/Hostess greets guest.

STEP 3:   Host/Hostess describes menu program and services.

STEP 4:   Counter server greets guest.

STEP 5:   Counter server presents menu and takes order.

STEP 6:   Counter server fills order.

TQS: Within 3 minutes.

STEP 7:   Counter server checks order with guest.

STEP 8:   Counter server completes guest check transaction.

STEP 9:   Self-service is used for condiments and tableware.

STEP 10:   Self-service is used for seating.

TQS: Table area clean.

STEP 11:   Server checks table.

   TQS: Offer Samples.

STEP 12:   Counter server explains menu items, takes dessert
and beverage order

   TQS: Within 1 minute.

STEP 13:   Counter server fills order.

   TQS: Within 3 minutes.

STEP 13 (ALTERNATE):   Counter server delivers to-go order.

STEP 14:   Counter server completes guest check transaction.

STEP 15:   Floor manager closes with guest.

ILLUSTRATED PATH OF SERVICE FOR QUICK FOOD STYLE RESTAURANT

SELF-SERVICE/COUNTER SERVICE

STEP 1: Guest is acknowledged.
TQS: Within 1 minute.

STEP 2: Host/Hostess greets guest.

STEP 3 : Host/Hostess describes menu services.

STEP 4 : Counter server greets guest.

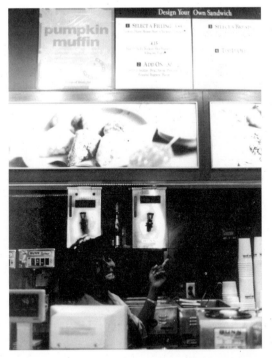

Step 5 : Counter server presents menu and takes order.

Step 6 : Counter server fills order.
TQS: *Within 3 minutes.*

STEP 7 : Counter server checks order with guest.

STEP 8 : Counter server completes guest check transaction.

STEP 9 : Self-service is used for condiments and tableware.

STEP 10 : Self-service is used for seating.

TQS: *Table area clean.*

STEP 11 : Server checks table.

TQS: *Offer samples.*

STEP 12 : Counter server explains menu items, takes dessert and beverage order.

TQS: *Within 1 minute.*

STEP 13 : Counter server fills order
TQS: *Within 3 minutes.*

STEP 13 (ALTERNATIVE): Counter server
fills to-go order.

STEP 14: Counter server completes guest check transaction.

STEP 15: Floor manager closes with guest.

WORKSHEET

CRITICAL PATH OF SERVICE QUICK FOOD STYLE RESTAURANT—SELF-SERVICE/COUNTER SERVICE

STEP 1: _____

STEP 2: _____

STEP 3: _____

STEP 4: _____

STEP 5: _____

STEP 6: _____

STEP 7: _____

STEP 8: _____

STEP 9: _____

STEP 10: _____

STEP 11: _____

STEP 12: _____

STEP 13: _____

STEP 14: _____

STEP 15: _____

CRITICAL PATH OF SERVICE OUTLINE
CASUAL FAMILY STYLE RESTAURANT—
RUNNER SERVICE

STEP 1:   Hostess/host greets guest.

STEP 2:   Hostess/host presents menu and seats guest.

STEP 3:   Server greets guest.

              TQS: _____

STEP 4:   Server describes menu and specials.

STEP 5:   Sever takes beverage and menu order.

STEP 6:   Server serves beverage order.

              TQS: _____

STEP 7:   Runner serves first course.

              TQS: ._____

STEP 8:   Server buses first course items, replenishes beverages.

STEP 9:   Runner serves second course.

              TQS: _____

STEP 10: Floor manager checks table.

STEP 11: Server buses second course item.

STEP 12: Server presents dessert menu.

STEP 13: Server serves coffee/final beverage.

STEP 13A: Server drops check if service is complete.

STEP 14: Server serves dessert course.

STEP 15: Server replenishes coffee/final beverage, and drops check.

STEP 16: Server picks up check.

TQS: _____

STEP 17: Server closes with guest.

STEP 18: Hostess/host closes with guest.

Grotto Restaurant

The Grotto Restaurant Company originally began as a pizza restaurant operation servicing the Southern Delaware beach resort community of Rehoboth. The restaurant menu now offers a range of items, including appetizers, soup and salad combinations, pizza, and other main course selections. The chain has grown to over 30 units and ranges from beachfront casual pizza and sandwich outlets to full service restaurants and sports bars. As seen in the photo illustration of Step 10, Total Quality Service points can be added with the simple addition of the server plating pizza slices for the guests before leaving it for continued self-service.

Appetizers

Grotto Pizza Jr.	2.95	Garlic Bread	1.95
each additional topping .75		with melted cheese	2.95
Grotto Pizza Jr. Bianco	3.95	Cheese Sticks	3.95
Chicken Tenders	4.75	Onion Rings	3.25
Spicy Chicken Wings	4.75	Nachos Supreme	4.95
Jalapeno Peppers	3.50	Crispy Corn Poppers	3.95
filled with cheddar cheese		with monterey jack cheese	
Boardwalk Fries	2.95	Broccoli & Cheese Bites	3.95
topped with cheddar	3.95	melted cheese & tasty broccoli	
		Fruit Cup (in season)	2.75

Soups & Salads

Fresh Tossed Salad............2.75
Soup du Jour............Cup 1.50....Bowl 2.95
Soup du Jour & Fresh Tossed Salad............3.95
French Onion Soup - Grotto's Famous............4.25
a steaming crock of traditional onion soup covered with toast and topped with lots of our own special cheese
Chili............Cup 1.95....Bowl 3.25
garnished with jalapeno pepper and shredded cheese

Tuna Salad	6.25	Turkey Breast Chef's Salad	6.25
freshly made tuna salad, served with crisp vegetables		all-white turkey breast, cheese, served on a bed of mixed salad greens, with fresh vegetables	
Chef's Salad	6.25	Chicken Breast Salad	6.25
imported ham, sliced turkey breast, salami, cheese, on a bed of mixed salad greens		charbroiled breast of chicken, served on a bed of mixed salad greens with fresh vegetables	
Antipasto	6.50	Pasta Salad	5.50
genoa salami, italian ham, pepperoni, provolone cheese, on a bed of mixed salad greens, with olives, peppers and fresh vegetables (anchovies on request)		a flavorful blend of rotini with a medley of fresh veggies	
		Fresh Fruit Salad (in season)	5.95
		a combo of fresh seasonal fruit	

Choice of Dressing
House Dressing
Italian • Ranch • French • Imported Olive Oil & Vinegar
1000 Island • Bleu Cheese

Side Orders

Boardwalk Fries	2.95	Spaghetti	2.95
topped with cheddar	3.95	Meatballs (2)	2.75
Cole Slaw	1.95	with melted cheese & Italian bread	
creamy homestyle		Garlic Bread	1.95
Pasta Salad	1.95	with melted cheese	2.95

Kids menu

for children 12 years old and under

Grotto Pizza Jr...........2.95   Spaghetti & Meatball...........2.95
includes kids size soda or milk

Kidsburger	2.50	Grilled Cheese	2.25
Hot Dog	2.25	Chicken Fingers	2.25
PB&J	1.75	Medley of Fresh Fruit	2.25

includes kids size soda or milk with french fries or applesauce

Soft Ice Cream   Shirley Temple
Cone or Cup...........1.00   or Roy Rogers...........1.00

• Kids; Why Not Celebrate Your Next Birthday With Us! •

PIZZA
Our Specialty

A family recipe using only the finest ingredients, and baked under the strictest controls by our skilled bakers.

The "legendary taste" combines crispy, tender crust made from home-made dough, real aged dairy cheeses and our own Grotto Pizza sauce.

	12" Small	16" Large
Plain Cheese	6.95	8.95

Toppings

Mushrooms	Pepperoni	Anchovies
Sausage	Extra Cheese	Green Peppers
Bacon	Meatballs	Black Olives

Each additional topping	1.80	1.90
Each additional half topping	.90	.95
Onion	1.50	1.50
Garlic		"No Charge"

Grotto Classics

The Everything "Bakers Choice"	13.75	16.75
includes pepperoni, mushrooms, green peppers, sausage, onion, garlic and extra cheese (anchovies on request, no substitutes)		
The Grande	12.95	15.95
two layers of dough filled with cheese, sauce, topping of your choice, onion, and just a hint of garlic—cheesy, thick, and delicious!		
Pizza Bianco	9.75	12.75
a white pizza—no tomato sauce, but plenty of cheese, oregano, basil, onion, garlic and fresh ground pepper, baked on a pan		
Bianco Olé	10.75	13.75
a bianco-style pizza made with sliced fresh tomatoes, red onions and jalapenos (optional, but highly recommended), baked on a pan		
Veggie Bianco	10.75	13.75
sliced fresh tomatoes, broccoli, mushrooms, black olives, red onions, a special blend of spices, and olive oil, baked on a pan		
Italian Tomato Pie (No Cheese)	9.75	12.75
lightly sauced, sliced fresh tomatoes, onion, garlic, olive oil and baked on a pan		
Grotto Pizza Junior		2.95
an 8" personal pizza just for you! each additional topping .75		
Grotto Pizza Junior Bianco		3.95
same as our regular bianco, but in an 8" personal size		

By the Slice

Plain Cheese	1.50	Bianco white pizza	2.00
1 topping	2.00	Grande (pepperoni only)	2.25
2 toppings	2.25		

Grotto Restaurant Menu.

Pasta - Pasta - Pasta

Spaghetti - Linguini - Ziti

Grotto Sauce	4.95	Meatballs	6.25
Grotto Marinara Sauce	4.95	White Clam Sauce	6.50

Pasta Specialties

Lasagna **6.50**
pasta layered with ricotta cheese and meat, our homemade sauce
and special blend of cheese

Cheese Manicotti **6.50**
a pasta crepe filled with ricotta cheese, topped with marinara sauce
and special blend of cheese

Cheese Ravioli **6.50**
filled with ricotta cheese, topped with our homemade sauce

Baked Ziti **6.50**
baked with marinara sauce and a special blend of cheese

Chicken Parmesan & Pasta **6.95**
chicken breast, marinara sauce & special blend of cheese, served with spaghetti

Submarines

cold subs include provolone, lettuce, tomato, pickles & onions

Italian Sub **5.75**
capicola, genoa salami,
pepper ham

Turkey Sub **5.75**
all-white turkey breast, mayo

Ham Sub **5.75**
imported danish ham

Tuna Sub **5.75**
all-white tuna, mayo

Cheese Steak **5.75**
philly style, ask for: onions, lettuce,
sweet or hot peppers, tomatoes
(mushrooms or extra cheese .90)

Meatball Sub **5.25**
in our homemade sauce,
with melted provolone cheese

Cheese Sub **5.75**
cheddar, american, provolone

Roast Beef Sub **5.95**
thinly sliced tender roast beef, mayo

***Cheezee* Cheese Steak** ..**6.95**
philly style steak with cheese galore
(american, provolone, cheddar)

Pizza Cheese Steak **6.25**
philly style steak with Grotto sauce,
pepperoni & our special blend of cheese

House Sandwich - French Dip **5.95**
thinly sliced juicy roast beef piled high on a
french roll, served with au jus

Chicken Parmesan Sandwich ...**5.25**
tender breast of chicken, marinara sauce
& cheese, served on fresh italian bread

Make-It-Great

from our Charbroiler

Grotto Burger **3.95**
1/2 lb. of fresh ground beef (cooked to order)

Hot Dog **1.50**
an American favorite

Breast of Chicken **4.50**
100% real chicken breast

(lettuce, tomato, pickle, raw onion on request)

Toppings add 50¢

Cheddar	Swiss	Mozzarella	Sautéed Onions
Provolone	American	Homestyle Chili	Sautéed Mushrooms

Make It Greater as a platter

Seasoned Fries & Homestyle Cole Slaw for additional $2.00

Ice Cream

creamy luscious soft serve

	small	large
Cone or Cup	1.75	1.95
Super Waffle Cone		2.50

Sundaes

Hot Fudge Nut ....*A Grotto Favorite* **2.95**
ice cream topped with hot fudge, whipped cream,
nuts and a cherry

Butterscotch **2.75**
Strawberry **2.75**

Other Sweet Treats

Cheesecake **1.95**
Snickers Pie **2.95**
Reeses Pieces Pie **2.95**

Beverages Coca-Cola CLASSIC

	Small	Medium	Large
Soft Drinks	1.25	1.50	1.75

Coke, Diet Coke, Sprite, Birch Beer, Hi-C Fruit Punch, Lemonade, Iced Tea

Pitcher of Soda or **Lipton** Iced Tea	3.50
Guzzler (Grotto souvenir cup)	2.75
Evian Natural Spring Water	1.75
Hot Coffee or Tea (Free refills)	.85
Hot Chocolate	1.00
Milk	1.25

Delaware Law Requires Persons to be 21 Years of Age in Order to Consume
Alcoholic Beverages. We Will Ask For I.D.

Draft Beer

icy and refreshing, served in a frosted mug

	Mug	Pitcher
Budweiser	1.95	7.50
Miller Genuine Draft	1.95	7.50
Coors Light, Miller Lite	1.95	7.50
Heineken		Bottle 3.25
O'Douls (Non-Alcoholic)		Bottle 1.75

House Wine

COPPERIDGE
ERNEST & JULIO GALLO

	Glass	1/2 Carafe	Carafe
Cabernet Sauvignon	2.25	3.95	6.50
White Zinfandel	2.50	4.95	8.50
Chardonnay	2.50	4.95	8.50
Chianti	2.50		Bottle 10.00
Riunite Lambrusco			Bottle 10.00

(Ask To See Our Wine List For Additional Choices)

Mixed Drinks

Frozen Strawberry Daiquiri ....*Grotto's Special* **5.25**
Luscious Strawberries & Bacardi Rum, topped with mounds of whipped cream

House Specialties **4.75**
Grotto Iced Tea, Planters Punch, Peaches & Cream

Frozen Drinks **5.25**
Peach Daiquiri, Margarita, Pina Colada

Frozen Strawberry Daiquiri or Pina Colada **4.25**
Non-Alcoholic

GROTTO RESTAURANT'S
APPLICATION OF CRITICAL PATH OF SERVICE OUTLINE
FOR CASUAL FAMILY STYLE RESTAURANT

STEP 1:   Hostess/host greets guest.

STEP 2:   Hostess/host presents menu and seats guest.

STEP 3:   Server greets guest.

TQS: Within 3 minutes.

STEP 4:   Server describes menu and specials.

STEP 5:   Server takes beverage and menu order.

STEP 6:   Server serves beverage order.

TQS: Within 3 minutes.

STEP 7:   Runner serves first course.

STEP 8:   Server buses first course.

STEP 9:   Runner serves main course.

STEP 10.   Server serves main course.

STEP 11:   Server replenishes beverage.

STEP 12:   Server buses main course.

STEP 13: Server presents dessert menu and takes dessert order.

STEP 14: Server buses glassware.

STEP 15: Server serves dessert course and coffee.

STEP 16: Server buses dessert course.

STEP 17: Server drops check and replenishes coffee.

STEP 18: Server picks up check.

TQS: Within 3 minutes.

STEP 19: Server replenishes coffee.

STEP 20: Server delivers to-go box and closes with guests.

STEP 21: Hostess/host closes with guest.

ILLUSTRATED PATH OF SERVICE
FOR CASUAL FAMILY STYLE RESTAURANT

STEP 1 : Hostess/host greets and seats guests.

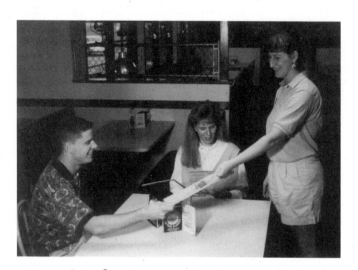

STEP 2 : Hostess presents menu.

STEP 3 : Server greets guests.

STEP 4 : Server describes menu and specials.

STEP 5 : Server takes beverage and menu order.

STEP 6: Server serves beverage order.
TQS: *Within 3 minutes.*

STEP 6a: First, server puts cocktail napkin down.

STEP 6b: Second, server places glass on table.

STEP 6c: Third, server pours wine.

STEP 6d: Fourth, server completes beverage order.

STEP 7 : Server serves first course.

STEP 7a: Server serves female guest first.

STEP 7b: Server serves male guest second.

STEP 8: Server buses first course.

STEP 8a: Server removes dishes from female guest first.

STEP 8b: Server removes dishes from male guest second.

S T E P 9 : Runner serves main course.

STEP 10 : Server serves main course.

STEP 10a: TQS point: *Server provides tableside plating service of pizza slices.*

STEP 10b : Sever serves male guest second..

STEP 11: Server replenishes beverage.

STEP 12: Server buses main course.

STEP 13: Server presents dessert menu and takes dessert order.

STEP 14: Server buses glassware.

STEP 15: Server serves dessert course and coffee.

STEP 16: Server buses dessert course.

STEP 17 : Server drops check and replenishes coffee.

STEP 18 : Server picks up check.

TQS: *Within 3 minutes.*

STEP 19: Server replenishes coffee.

STEP 20: Server delivers to-go box and closes with guests.

STEP 21 : Hostess/host closes with guest.

WORKSHEET

CRITICAL PATH OF SERVICE
CASUAL FAMILY STYLE RESTAURANT

STEP 1: ————————————————————————

STEP 2: ————————————————————————

STEP 3: ————————————————————————

STEP 4: ————————————————————————

STEP 5: ————————————————————————

STEP 6: ————————————————————————

STEP 7: ————————————————————————

STEP 8: ————————————————————————

STEP 9: ————————————————————————

STEP 10: ———————————————————————

STEP 11: ———————————————————————

STEP 12: ———————————————————————

STEP 13: ———————————————————————

STEP 14: ────────────────────────────────

STEP 15: ────────────────────────────────

STEP 16: ────────────────────────────────

STEP 17: ────────────────────────────────

STEP 18: ────────────────────────────────

CRITICAL PATH OF SERVICE OUTLINE
CASUAL STYLE RESTAURANT—BREAKFAST SERVICE

STEP 1:   Hostess/host greets and seats guest.

STEP 2:   Server greets guest, describes menu and specials.

STEP 3:   Server pours coffee and/or juice.

STEP 4:   Server takes breakfast order.

STEP 5:   Server serves breakfast beverages.

STEP 6:   Runner serves first course.

STEP 7:   Server buses first course.

STEP 9:   Server serves main course and drops check.

STEP 10: Floor manager checks table.

STEP 11: Server buses main course.

STEP 12: Server picks up check.

          TQS: _____

STEP 13: Server closes with guests.

STEP 14: Hostess/host closes with guest.

CRITICAL PATH OF SERVICE OUTLINE
CASUAL STYLE RESTAURANT—BUFFET BREAKFAST

STEP 1:   Hostess/host greets and seats guest.

STEP 2:   Server greets guest, and describes buffet.

STEP 3:   Server pours coffee.

STEP 4:   Server takes beverage order.

STEP 5:   Server serves breakfast beverages.

STEP 6:   Guest serves self from buffet.

STEP 7:   Server buses first course and replenishes coffee.

STEP 8:   Guest serves self from buffet.

STEP 9:   Server checks table and drops check.

STEP 10: Floor manager checks table.

STEP 11: Server buses main course.

STEP 13: Server picks up check.

TQS: _____

STEP 14: Server closes with guests.

STEP 15: Hostess/host closes with guest.

Breakfast in a large business hotel dining room is anything but relaxed. The primary motivation for most business customers is to get in and get out, unless a business breakfast meeting is in progress. Hotel companies such as Marriott, Hilton, and ITT Sheraton place a primary emphasis on quick service and quality food for breakfast service. Establishing critical steps of service for a breakfast wait staff can help to eliminate many of the customer complaints. For regular menu service orders the service steps that cause the most problems are:

- Getting the first cup of coffee to the customer
- Making sure that main course items are hot
- Dropping the check in a timely manner and completing the check transaction with the guest promptly

Buffet presentations have become the most common answer to customer complaints of slow breakfast service. Although fast for the guest and easy for the wait staff buffets present their own set of service problems:

- Reacting promptly to the service need of the customer
- Getting the first cup of coffee to the customer
- Charging the customer for the right level of buffet breakfast (many buffet breakfast programs offer three tiers of menu price selections: continental; cereal and fruit; and full breakfast)

- Dropping the check in a timely manner and completing the check transaction with the guest promptly

The critical path of buffet service helps wait staff to understand that service steps still need to be consistently performed in order for customers to experience Total Quality Service.

GARDEN ROOM APPLICATION OF
CRITICAL PATH OF SERVICE OUTLINE FOR
CASUAL STYLE RESTAURANT—BREAKFAST SERVICE

STEP 1:   Hostess/host greets guest.

STEP 2:   Hostess/host seats guest, describes menu and specials.

STEP 3:   Server greets guest, pours coffee, and takes breakfast beverage order.

STEP 4:   Server serves breakfast beverages.

STEP 5:   Server takes breakfast order.

STEP 6:   Server serves first course.

STEP 7:   Server buses first course.

STEP 8:   Server serves main course.

STEP 9:   Server drops check.

STEP 10: Floor manager checks table.

    TQS: *Offers muffin.*

STEP 11: Server buses main course.

STEP 12: Server picks up check and replenishes beverages.

STEP 13: Server completes check transaction and closes with guests.

TQS: *Within 3 minutes.*

STEP 14: Hostess/host closes with guest.

ILLUSTRATED PATH OF SERVICE
FOR CASUAL STYLE RESTAURANT— BREAKFAST SERVICE

STEP 1: Hostess/host greets guest.

STEP 2: Hostess/host seats guest, describes menu and specials.

STEP 3: Server greets guest, pours coffee, and takes breakfast beverage order.

STEP 4: Server serves breakfast beverages.

STEP 5: Server takes breakfast order.

STEP 6: Server serves first course.

STEP 7 : Server buses first course.

STEP 8 : Server serves main course.

STEP 9 : Server drops check.

STEP 10 : Floor manager checks table.
TQS: *Offers muffin.*

STEP 11 : Server buses main course.

STEP 12 : Server picks up check and replenishes beverages.

STEP 13 : Server completes check transaction and closes with guests.
TQS: *Within 3 minutes.*

STEP 14 : Hostess/host closes with guest.

WORKSHEET

CRITICAL PATH OF SERVICE
CASUAL STYLE RESTAURANT—BREAKFAST SERVICE

STEP 1: ————————————————————————

STEP 2: ————————————————————————

STEP 3: ————————————————————————

STEP 4: ————————————————————————

STEP 5: ————————————————————————

STEP 6: ————————————————————————

STEP 7: ————————————————————————

STEP 8: ————————————————————————

STEP 9: ————————————————————————

STEP 10: ————————————————————————

STEP 11: ————————————————————————

STEP 12: ————————————————————————

STEP 13: ————————————————————————

STEP 14: ————————————————————————

STEP 15: ————————————————————————

WORKSHEET

CRITICAL PATH OF SERVICE
CASUAL STYLE RESTAURANT: BUFFET BREAKFAST

STEP 1: ─────────────────────────────────

STEP 2: ─────────────────────────────────

STEP 3: ─────────────────────────────────

STEP 4: ─────────────────────────────────

STEP 5: ─────────────────────────────────

STEP 6: ─────────────────────────────────

STEP 7: ─────────────────────────────────

STEP 8: ─────────────────────────────────

STEP 9: ─────────────────────────────────

STEP 10: ────────────────────────────────

STEP 11: ────────────────────────────────

STEP 12: ────────────────────────────────

STEP 13: ────────────────────────────────

STEP 14: ────────────────────────────────

STEP 15: ────────────────────────────────

CRITICAL PATH OF SERVICE OUTLINE

FULL-SERVICE RESTAURANT—BISTRO STYLE DINNER SERVICE

STEP 1:   Hostess/host greets guests.

STEP 2:   Hostess/host seats guests and presents menu.

STEP 3:   Server greets guest.

TQS: _____

STEP 4:   Server describes menu and specials.

STEP 5:   Server takes beverage order.

STEP 6:   Server serves beverage order.

TQS: _____

STEP 7:   Server takes menu order.

STEP 8:   Server takes wine order.

STEP 9:   Server serves hot bread.

STEP 10: Server serves wine.

STEP 11: Server serves first course.

TQS: _____

STEP 12: Server buses first course and replenishes beverages.

STEP 13: Server serves second course.

       TQS: _____

STEP 14: Server replenishes beverages.

STEP 15: Server buses second course items.

STEP 16: Server serves main course.

STEP 17: Server replenishes beverages.

STEP 18: Floor manager checks table.

STEP 19: Server buses main course.

STEP 20: Server presents dessert menu.

STEP 21: Server takes dessert order.

STEP 22: Server serves coffee.

STEP 23: Server serves dessert course.

STEP 24: Server replenishes coffee and drops check if service is complete.

STEP 25: Server buses dessert course.

STEP 25: Server serves after dinner drink.

STEP 26: Server presents check.

STEP 27: Server picks up check.

STEP 28: Server closes with guest.

STEP 29: Hostess/host closes with guest.

■ THE REUNION INN & GRILL

The Reunion Inn & Grill in Camden, Maine, is a full-service restaurant offering a bistro atmosphere. The building, a converted weaving mill, provides a large open space with high ceilings, exposed wood beams, and wide plank natural oak floors. 12 over 12 pane windows provide ample natural light. The kitchen takes up one end of the building, a bar occupies the center section, and table seating for approximately 50 guests fills the balance of floor space. Upstairs six sleeping rooms and a private banquet room complete the facilities.

The menu offers a range of regional American cuisine items focusing on fresh fish and shellfish. Average check without alcohol is $24 per person for dinner. The service atmosphere is informal. Guests are encouraged to select courses in any order that they choose, providing service challenges for the staff and requiring a flexible and relaxed attitude toward service steps. "Whatever it takes" is a service policy appropriate to this operation.

Reunion Inn & Grill

THE REUNION INN & GRILL APPLICATION OF CRITICAL PATH OF SERVICE OUTLINE FOR FULL-SERVICE RESTAURANT— BISTRO STYLE DINNER SERVICE

STEP 1:   Hostess/host greets guests.

STEP 2:   Hostess/host seats guests and presents menu.

STEP 3:   Server greets guests and serves hot breads.

TQS: Within 3 minutes.

STEP 4:   Server describes menu and specials.

STEP 5:   Server takes beverage order.

STEP 6:   Server serves beverage order.

TQS: Within 3 minutes.

STEP 7:   Server takes menu order.

STEP 8:   Server serves first course.

STEP 9:   Server buses first course items.

STEP 10: Server serves second course.

STEP 11: Server buses second course items.

STEP 12: Server presents wines and takes wine order.

TQS: *Marry wines to menu order.*

STEP 13: Server serves wine.

STEP 14: Server serves main course.

STEP 15: Chef/floor manager checks table.

STEP 16: Server replenishes wine.

STEP 17: Server replenishes water.

STEP 18: Server buses main course and takes dessert order.

STEP 19: Server serves dessert course.

STEP 20: Server serves coffee.

STEP 21: Server replenishes coffee and drops check if service is complete.

STEP 22: Server buses dessert course.

STEP 23: Server completes dessert course service and takes beverage order.

STEP 24: Server serves after dinner drink.

STEP 25: Server presents check.

STEP 26: Server picks up check and closes with guest.

TQS: *Within 3 minutes.*

STEP 27: Hostess/host closes with guests.

ILLUSTRATED PATH OF SERVICE FOR FULL-SERVICE RESTAURANT—BISTRO STYLE DINNER SERVICE

STEP 1: Hostess/host greets guests.

STEP 2: Hostess/host seats guests and presents menu.

Step 3: Server greets guests and serves hot breads.
     TQS: *Within 3 minutes.*

Step 4: Server describes menu and specials.

Step 5: Server takes beverage order.

STEP 6 : Server serves beverage order.

STEP 7 : Server takes menu order.

STEP 8: Server serves first course.

STEP 8a: Server serves female guest first.

STEP 8b: Server serves male guest second.

Step 9: Server buses first course items.

Step 9a: Server removes dish from female guest first.

Step 9b: Server removes dish from male guest second.

STEP 10: Server serves second course.

STEP 10a: Server serves female guest first.

STEP 10b: Server serves male guest second.

STEP 11 : Server buses second course items.

STEP 11a: Server removes dish from female guest first.

STEP 11b: Server removes dish from fmale guest second.

STEP 12: Server presents wines and takes wine order.

STEP 13: Server serves wine.

STEP 14: Server serves main course.

STEP 14a: Server serves to the right of the guest with the right hand.

STEP 14b: Server serves male guest second.

STEP 15 : Chef/floor manager checks table.

STEP 16 : Server replenishes wine.

STEP 17 : Server replenishes water.

STEP 18 : Server buses main course and takes dessert order.

STEP 19 : Server serves dessert course.

STEP 20 : Server serves coffee.

STEP 21 : Server replenishes coffee and drops check if service is complete.

STEP 22 : Server buses dessert course.

STEP 23 : Server completes dessert course service and takes
        beverage order.

STEP 24: Server serves after dinner drink.

STEP 24a: Server serves female guest first.

STEP 24b: Server serves beverages to the right of the guest with the right hand.

STEP 25 : Server presents check.

STEP 26 : Server picks up check and closes with guest.
TQS: *Within 3 minutes.*

STEP 27 : Hostess/host closes with guests.

CRITICAL PATH OF SERVICE
FULL-SERVICE RESTAURANT—BISTRO STYLE
DINNER SERVICE

STEP 1: _____

STEP 2: _____

STEP 3: _____

STEP 4: _____

STEP 5: _____

STEP 6: _____

STEP 7: _____

STEP 8: _____

STEP 9: _____

STEP 10: _____

STEP 11: _____

STEP 12: _____

STEP 13: _____

STEP 14: _____

STEP 15: _____

STEP 16: _____

STEP 17: _____

STEP 18: _____

STEP 19: _____

STEP 20: _____

STEP 21: _____

STEP 22: _____

STEP 23: _____

STEP 24: _____

STEP 25: _____

STEP 26: _____

STEP 27: _____

CRITICAL PATH OF SERVICE OUTLINE

FULL-SERVICE TRADITIONAL DINNER SERVICE

STEP 1: Host/hostess greets guests.

STEP 2: Server greets guest.

STEP 3: Server presents menu and describes specials.

STEP 4: Server takes beverage orders.

STEP 5: Bus person pours water.

STEP 6: Server serves beverage orders (TQS point).

STEP 7: Server takes menu and wine orders.

STEP 8: Bus person serves hot breads.

STEP 9: Server serves first course.

STEP 10: Bus person buses first course item.

STEP 11: Server serves second course.

STEP 12: Server serves wine.

STEP 13: Bus person replenishes water.

STEP 14: Server serves wine.

STEP 15: Bus person buses main course. (TQS point)

STEP 16: Server presents dessert menu/takes dessert order.

STEP 17: Server serves coffee.

STEP 18: Server serves dessert course.

STEP 19: Server replenishes coffee/takes after dinner drink order.

STEP 20: Bus person buses dessert courses.

STEP 21: Server serves after dinner drink.

STEP 22: Server presents check.

STEP 23: Server picks up check. (TQS point)

STEP 24: Server closes with guest.

STEP 25: Host/hostess closes with guest.

Ruth Chris Steak House, Philadelphia, Pennsylvania.

Ruth's Chris Steak House interior.

The service at the Ruth's Chris Steak House in center city Philadelphia is more in the tradition of the classical style of full-service dining. The wait staff consist of a principal server, a runner, and a bus person. This is the classical front waiter/back waiter and bus person combination of formal French table service. The photographs that illustrate this section clearly identify that the dining experience will be gracious and comfortable. Servers are attentive, prompt, and relaxed.

The menu focuses on steak with a large variety of side items served in generous portions. Atmosphere and service should reflect the value of the $45 average check per person without alcohol.

APPETIZERS & SOUPS

Barbecued Shrimp—Awarded *"Best of Philly"*	9.95	Maryland Lump Crab Cake	8.95
Shrimp La Louisiane	8.25	Island Fried Shrimp with Marmalade	9.95
Shrimp Cocktail	8.25	Escargot with Artichoke Hearts	7.95
Shrimp Remoulade	8.25	French Fried Onion Rings	3.95
Mushrooms Stuffed with Crabmeat	7.95	Fried Calamari	8.95
Onion Soup Au Gratin	4.25	Fried Ricotta Over Fresh Tomatoes and Basil	8.95

SALADS

Italian	4.50	Spinach	4.95
Combination	3.95	Heart of Lettuce	3.75
Sliced Tomato	3.95	Fresh Asparagus	5.95
Sliced Tomato and Onion	4.25	Caesar	5.95
Shrimp Caesar	11.95		

Dressings: Our House Specialty is Sicilian; we also offer Bleu Cheese, Remoulade, Thousand Island, Ranch, Creole French, Hot Bacon, Italian and Honey Mustard. (All made fresh daily from our exclusive recipes.)

CLASSIC SAUCES

Hollandaise, Béarnaise, Bordelaise and Au Poivre	2.50

PRIME BEEF AND BLEU CHEESE

Select any one of our U.S. Prime Steaks, and we'll top it with a generous
portion of richly aged bleu cheese.   (additional) .95

POTATOES

Baked (large, moist and firm for our steak lovers)	3.00	Lyonnaise (sautéed with Onions)	3.50
		Steak Fries (big and rough cut)	3.50
Baked (with butter, sour cream, bacon & chives)	3.50	Julienne (fried long and thin)	3.50
		Shoestring (fried crispy, cut extra-thin)	3.50
Au Gratin (in cream sauce, topped with thick melted sharp cheddar)	4.75	Cottage (thick round slices)	3.50
		Fresh Potato Chips	3.50
		Homemade Mashed Potatoes	3.50

VEGETABLES

Fresh Broccoli or Cauliflower	3.75	Sautéed Mushrooms	3.95
Au Gratin	4.75	French Fried Onion Rings	3.95
Creamed Spinach	3.75	Fresh Asparagus	5.95
Au Gratin	4.75	with Hollandaise	6.75
Broiled Tomatoes	3.75		

DESSERTS

Blueberry or Fresh Strawberry Cheesecake	3.95	Fresh Strawberries	4.95
		Mississippi Mud Pie	4.95
Chocolate Mousse Cheesecake	3.95	Key Lime Pie	4.95
Fresh Strawberries with Sweet Cream Sauce	5.25	Chocolate Fantasy Cake	4.95
		Bread Pudding with Whiskey Sauce	3.95
Caramel Custard	3.95	Selection of Ice Creams	3.95
Pecan Pie	3.95	Warm Apple Tart with	
A La Mode	4.95	Vanilla Ice Cream	4.95

COFFEES

Espresso	2.95	Cappuccino	3.50

Sorry, no separate checks.
Inquire about our gift certificates—personal and corporate charge accounts—rooms for private parties.

PHIL394

Ruth's Chris Steak House Menu.

ABOUT YOUR STEAK: Your steak at Ruth's Chris Steak House is THE finest in the U.S. Your steak here is a large portion of aged, corn-fed Midwestern beef. Never frozen, it is hand-cut here, broiled to your specifications and served sizzling in butter.

RARE Very red, cool center. **MEDIUM RARE** Red, warm center. **MEDIUM** Pink center.
MEDIUM WELL Slightly pink center. **WELL** Broiled throughout, no pink.

FILET
21.95
A thick cut of the tenderest corn-fed Midwestern beef.
So tender it practically melts in your mouth.

PETITE FILET
18.50
A smaller, but equally tender filet.

RIBEYE
19.95
An outstanding example of U.S. Prime at its best. This steak has the most
marbling of all prime cuts, which makes the ribeye flavorful and tender.

NEW YORK STRIP
23.95
This specially aged U.S. Prime sirloin strip is the favorite of many steak connoisseurs.
It is a little firmer than a ribeye, and has a full-bodied flavor.

PORTERHOUSE (for 2 persons)
(per person) 27.95
A massive cut of the finest U.S. Prime beef, suitable for sharing, combining the
rich flavor of the strip steak with the tenderness of the filet.

CENTER CUT PORK CHOPS
16.75
Two 10 oz. center cut chops. Extra-fine grained and flavorful. Broiled to
perfection, served sizzling with sweet and spicy apple slices.

LAMB CHOPS
23.95
Two double cut chops, hand cut extra thick. Extremely tender, thanks
to the natural marbling. Broiled to perfection and served sizzling, with mint jelly.

PRIME VEAL CHOP
22.95
White milk-fed veal, the tender veal Europe loves. This chop is so delicately
flavored we simply broil it to release all the flavor, then serve it sizzling.

CHICKEN MARINADA
15.95
Fresh double breast of chicken, marinated, seasoned with herbs and broiled to perfection.

DUCK ORLEANS
21.95
Boneless one-half duck roasted crisp, glazed with orange brandied sauce
and served over Cajun rice.

FRESH LOBSTER
Market Price
Fresh live Maine lobster, ranging from 3 pounds and up, flown in daily.
If you'd like, select your own lobster from Ruth's Chris Tank.

SALMON FILET
19.95
The aristocrat of salmon, caught in cold waters.
Broiled or grilled to perfection.

TROUT PECAN
18.95
Filet of trout, topped with meuniere sauce and roasted pecans.

 Our steaks are served sizzling in butter, specify extra butter or none.

RUTH'S CHRIS STEAK HOUSE APPLICATION OF CRITICAL PATH OF SERVICE FOR FULL-SERVICE RESTAURANT—TRADITIONAL DINNER SERVICE

STEP 1:   Hostess/host greets and seats guests.

STEP 2:   Server greets guests and presents menu.

TQS: Within 3 minutes.

STEP 3:   Server describes specials.

STEP 4:   Server takes beverage order.

STEP 5:   Bus person serves water.

STEP 6:   Bus person serves hot breads.

STEP 7:   Server serves beverage order.

TQS: Within 5 minutes.

STEP 8:   Server takes menu order.

STEP 9:   Server takes wine order.

STEP 10: Runner serves first course.

STEP 11: Runner buses first course items.

STEP 12: Runner serves second course.

TQS: Provide pepper service.

STEP 13: Runner buses second course.

STEP 14: Bus person replenishes water.

STEP 15: Bus person replaces eating utensils.

(TQS Point)

STEP 16: Server serves wine.

STEP 17: Server serves main course.

TQS: Provide pepper service.

STEP 18: Server replenishes wine.

STEP 19: Bus person buses main course.

STEP 20: Bus person replaces eating utensils.

(TQS Point)

STEP 21: Server presents dessert menu and takes dessert order.

STEP 22: Server serves coffee.

STEP 23: Server serves dessert course.

STEP 24: Server replenishes coffee and takes after dinner drink order.

STEP 25: Bus person buses dessert course.

STEP 26: Server serves after dinner drink.

STEP 27: Server presents check.

STEP 28: Server picks up check.

TQS: Within 3 minutes.

STEP 29: Server closes with guests.

TQS: Offer long stem rose.

STEP 30: Hostess/host closes with guests.

ILLUSTRATED PATH OF SERVICE FOR FULL-SERVICE RESTAURANT— TRADITIONAL DINNER SERVICE

STEP 1: Hostess/host greets and seats guests.

STEP 2 : Server greets guests and presents menu.
TQS: *Within 3 minutes.*

STEP 3 : Server describes specials.

STEP 4 : Server takes beverage order.

STEP 5 : Bus person serves water.

STEP 6: Bus person serves hot breads.

STEP 7: Server serves beverage order.

TQS: *Within 5 minutes.*

STEP 8: Server takes menu order.

STEP 9: Server takes wine order.

STEP 10: Runner serves first course.

STEP 11: Runner buses first course items.

STEP 12: Runner serves second course.

TQS: *Provide pepper service.*

STEP 13: Runner buses second course.

STEP 14: Bus person replenishes water.

STEP 15: Bus person replaces eating utensils.
TQS: *Point*

STEP 16: Server serves wine.

STEP 17: Server serves main course.

STEP 17a: Server serves female guest first.

STEP 17b: Server serves male guest second.

STEP 17c: Server serves items surrounding main course.

STEP 17d: TQS: *Provide pepper service.*

STEP 18: Server replenishes wine.

STEP 19 : Bus person buses main course.

STEP 20 : Bus person replaces eating utensils.
TQS: *Point*

STEP 21 : Server presents dessert menu and takes dessert order.

STEP 22 : Server serves coffee.

STEP 22a: Server places coffee cup in front of guest.

STEP 22b: Server pours coffee.

STEP 23: Server serves dessert course.

STEP 23a: Server serves female guest first.

STEP 23b: Server serves male guest second.

STEP 24 : Server replenishes coffee and takes after dinner drink order.

STEP 25 : Bus person buses dessert course.

STEP 26 : Server serves after dinner drink.

STEP 27 : Server presents check.

STEP 28 : Server picks up check.

TQS: *Within 3 minutes.*

STEP 29 : Server closes with guests.

TQS: *Offer long stem rose.*

STEP 30: Hostess/host closes with guests.

WORKSHEET

CRITICAL PATH OF SERVICE
FULL-SERVICE RESTAURANT—
TRADITIONAL STYLE DINNER SERVICE

STEP 1: _____

STEP 2: _____

STEP 3: _____

STEP 4: _____

STEP 5: _____

STEP 6: _____

STEP 7 _____

STEP 8: _____

STEP 9: _____

STEP 10: _____

STEP 11: _____

STEP 12: _____

STEP 13: _____

STEP 14: _____

STEP 15: _____

STEP 16: _____

STEP 17: _____

STEP 18: _____

STEP 19: _____

STEP 20: _____

STEP 21: _____

STEP 22: _____

STEP 23: _____

STEP 24: _____

STEP 25: _____

STEP 26: _____

STEP 27: _____

STEP 28: _____

STEP 29: _____

STEP 30: _____

GUARANTEEING QUALITY SERVICE

The "guarantee" in the title of this book, *Quality Restaurant Service Guaranteed*, is not an overstatement or an erroneous marketing effort. It is, rather, a challenge to every foodservice operator, owner, and manager, asserting that "quality customer service" can be obtained and maintained in your business.

Throughout these pages the attempt has been made to outline a blueprint for designing and creating a quality service training program that, when implemented, cannot fail to supply employees with the necessary tools to provide quality service. It should not fail if it includes an honest evaluation of your operation, an accurate assessment of your customers, a realistic determination of the capabilities of your service staff and a thorough analysis of the minute details of the style of table service that is being offered to your customers.

It will fail, however, if one major factor is overlooked in the hiring and training of your service staff...attitude. Look through the illustrated paths of service for each style of operation and notice the commonality in all of them. Service staff are sincerely happy to serve their customers. The expressions on these servers' faces are genuine, as are their body attitudes in paying attention to the customers' needs. These are not models, hired for an afternoon photo shoot, but live and real time service staff for each of the profiled foodservice operations. What makes these illustrations accurate is the attitude of the service staff, the key ingredient to both their and your success.

The most pressing problem facing foodservice operators today, and in the future, is finding the staff to service your customers. The cost of hiring and training new employees averages $600.

Putting the critical path of service into action will require a training program and training calendar. An extended period of four to six weeks should be set aside to effectively allow time for all of your staff to be trained. This time period allows for foodservices operations that serve customers six and seven days a week to cover all of their employees while still covering breakfast, lunch, and dinner shift schedules. The following sample training calendar offers a guideline to implementing training for the implementation of a successful critical path of service.

TRAINING CALENDAR: TOTAL QUALITY SERVICE
FOUR WEEK CYCLE PROGRAM

SUNDAY	MONDAY	TUESDAY	WEDNESDAY	THURSDAY	FRIDAY	SATURDAY
						1 Staff Meeting
2 Training Cycle 1: <u>Service</u>	3	4	5	6	7	8 Post Comment Cards
9 Training Cycle 2: Product <u>Knowledge</u>	10	11	12	13	14	15 Post Team Incentive Results
16 Training Cycle 3: <u>Beverage</u>	17	18	19	20	21	22 Staff Meeting: Mid – Program Awards
23 Training Cycle 4: <u>Total Quality Sales & Service</u>	24	25	26	27	28	29 Post Team Incentive Results
30	31 Staff Awards Program					

BIBLIOGRAPHY

Alberta Tourism Educational Council Standards and Certification Initiative. Alberta, Canada: Alberta Tourism Education Council, 1992.

Albrecht, Karl. *At America's Service.* New York: Warner Books, 1988.

The Only Thing That Matters. New York: Harper Collins, 1992.

Albrecht, Karl and Lawrence Bradford. *The Service Advantage.* Homewood, Illinois: Dow Jones-Irwin, 1990.

Auer, J. T. *The Joy of Selling.* Holbrook, Massachusetts: Bob Adams, 1989.

Brown, Stanley. *Total Quality Service.* Scarborough, Ontario, Canada: Prentice Hall, 1992.

Carr, Clay. *The New Manager's Survival Manual.* New York: John Wiley, 1989.

Covey, Stephen. *The Seven Habits of Highly Effective People.* New York: Simon & Schuster, 1989.

Crosby, Philip. *Quality Without Tears*. New York: McGraw-Hill, 1984.

Drucker, Peter. *Innovation and Entrepreneurship*. New York: Harper & Row, 1986.

The New Realities. New York: Harper & Row, 1989.

Marvin, Bill. *Restaurant Basics*. New York: John Wiley, 1992.

Peters, Tom. *The Tom Peters Seminar*. New York: Vintage Books, 1994.

Tunks, Roger. *Fast Track to Quality*. New York: McGraw-Hill, 1992.

Zemke, Ron and Dick Schaaf. *The Service Edge*. New York: Penguin Group, 1989.

INDEX

Product:
   demands for, 4
   development, 41
   preparation and presentation, 8
   timely delivery of, 8–9
Profits, increase in, 15, 16
Puleri, Dominick, 25

Q
Quality:
   of American products, customer dissatisfaction with, 3
   consistency of, 8–11
   food, 17, 23, 47, 53, 65
      versus profit, 4
Quality service, 17, 53, 56
   evaluating efforts to establish, 59
   guaranteeing, 11, 65, 195–196
   search for, 3–4
Quality service points, 56, 59, 61
Quick service operations, 59–60, 75. *See also* Au Bon Pain
   critical path of service outline, 79–80
   worksheet 93–94

R
Refunds, 10
Repair, 3, 5, 7
Returns, 5, 7, 9
Reunion Inn & Grill (Camden, ME), 77, 136, *137*
   critical path of service outline, 138–140
   illustrated Critical Path of Service, *141–157*
Revenue, goals, 16, 47
Roses, 168, *187*
Runner, 95, 100, *108,* 118,163, 166, 167, *175–176*
   service, *see* Casual family style service
Ruth Chris' Steak House, 76, *162,* 163